THE COSMIC JOURNEY

A STARGAZER'S ODYSSEY

MANYA BAID

Chapter 1
Welcome to my Book-i-verse

"Thirty rupees for one kilo of potatoes. Thirty for one. Fresh Potatoes".

Twelve-year-old Ananta was on her way back home from school. She could hear the vegetable vendors crying at the top of their lungs in a rhythmic tone, on the streets of the small town of Faridabad. The garden blossomed with Hibiscus flowers and as she walked home, she could taste the delicious smell of the colorful flowers on her tongue.

Using the back door to enter her house, Ananta avoided the commotion and clatter of the streets. Exhausted, all she wished for was a stress-free and good day at school. Since middle school started, most days for her had been strenuous and wearing. However, this day in particular was one of the most distressing and heart-rending ones she's ever had. She couldn't help but look back at that one particular incident.

It was the last period of the day and sadly, it was physics. Ananta's classmates were screaming, fighting, eating, running about - acting as if the man had never evolved from the Hominids. Among the uncivilized loose cannons present in a so-called civilized educational institution, Ananta sat in the corner reading her science book.

Ananta's saving grace was the book kept neatly on her lap. Tuning out the white noise of the classroom, she opened the book. The next chapter in the eighth-grade syllabus was, perhaps, her favorite one. It was about stars and the solar system. Her fascination with space extended beyond just her school curricula as she had developed an interest in the same since a young age. Sometimes, it felt like her bond and love for the subject was stronger than her relationship with her parents or friends. And sometimes, it felt like this was her true calling -her future. Her dream was to become an astrophysicist, to explore the realms of the unknown and define infinity.

The teacher entered and the students stood up to greet the teacher.

A few minutes into the lesson Ananta was already lost in the vast sea of knowledge of astrophysics. Towards the end of the lesson, there was a quiz. Suddenly, it was Ananta's turn to answer. The teacher asked her about the distance between the earth and the sun. She knew the precise answer- 150.9 million km.

However, something stopped her from answering. The stares and whispers of the kids, the teacher's dreadful glare, the lights buzzing, the fan's noisy motion- it was all too much for her. If only there was a way people could see in her mind and help her unravel the tangled web of thoughts.

Before she could compose herself, someone from behind

shouted "USELESS"! Sure, Ananta was used to these taunts but, was that all she was, an insignificant being with no future or purpose in life? Just a minute particle on this floating rock, invisible to others, living a meaningful existence.

Upon reaching home, Ananta kept her school bag on the bed and sat down at her study table. Once again, unlike any other day, this was too distressing. Ananta had now given up hope altogether. She lay her head down on the table, exhausted from her monotonous routine. All she wished for was an escape from the voices in her head constantly tormenting her. Whenever she wanted to clear her head, she went to her dad's library and picked up her favorite book 'The Big Book of the Universe'; the book that always helped her calm down. The book was an encyclopedia of the universe containing information about the solar system, exoplanets, galaxies, stars, dark matter, black holes, quasars, accretion disks, singularity, and whatnot. It was her fortress of solitude. She flipped through the pages, with a glimmer in her eyes. She felt at peace. The voices in her head had gone silent.

However, something was quite peculiar. Flipping through the pages, she could feel the vibrations of the words on the pages passing through her body - through her arms, to her shoulders, to her neck, to her ears.

Chapter 2
The Solar Symphony

A cosmic giant lay in front of her. The brilliant white light emitted off of it blinded her for a second.

She couldn't recognize the celestial body when suddenly she heard a distorted voice behind her. A voice so eerie that it sent shivers down her spine. However, she could recognize the voice - it was the one and only Neil Tyson. Ananta suddenly realized that she was listening to his podcast on YouTube and fell asleep while doing so.

"What you're seeing is not just any ordinary celestial body", announced the voice, "It's the Sun".

"The SUN?", exclaimed Ananta. She always believed that the sun was a luminous, orange body. Well, at least that's what every student was taught.

"Disappointed, aren't you?" said the voice mockingly.

Ananta was surprised that the voice could read her mind. "Well yes, I believed that the sun was glaring yellow. How is this even possible?"

"Well my child, as we know, the atmosphere of space can't scatter light. So, without scattering we won't be able to see any other color except white light. In conclusion, the sun is white as seen in space." answered the voice.

 Ananta was baffled. This revelation led her to question if her was entire life a lie. Intrigued, she asked "Then what is the truth? Is the sun even real? Do we exist?" Ananta now had several unanswered questions.

"Patience my child, curiosity has its own reason for existing, but we must cultivate the habit of waiting patiently for the solutions. Come, let me quench your thirst for knowledge", said the voice in a gentle tone. That soft tone made Ananta feel like she had known the voice for eternity.

"The sun, also known as the center of the Milky Way Galaxy, is essentially a 4.6 billion-year-old dwarf star with a diameter of about 1.3927 million kilometers, weighing $1.988 * 10^{30}$ kgs," informed her voice.

"Well how do you calculate the mass of the sun?" questioned Ananta.

"You can calculate it using Kepler's third law i.e. $T^2 = 4\pi^2 r^3 / GM$ (sun). Substituting the values of the time period, the radius of the sun, and the gravitational constant, we can calculate the sun's mass."

"Oooh, that is interesting. I have another question. How is the sun a dwarf star?"

"I do get this question a lot. The sun is a star that is in its middle ages, commonly known as the main sequence. In this stage, the hydrogen in the core of the star is converted into helium by the process of fusion. This is when the two nuclei of the hydrogen atoms come together to react to form an atom of helium. The burning of hydrogen and helium in the core is an exothermic process i.e. it generates a lot of energy. This is the reason why the core of the sun is flaming hot," informed the voice.

"Don't stars die as well?" Ananta had a lot of questions in her mind. No one had ever encouraged her curiosity. She was always silenced for expressing her interest in learning but for the first time in her life she felt heard.

"Of course they do! Nothing is permanent in life; everything has to come to an end. So do stars, and it's a wonderful process. When a high-mass star has no hydrogen left to burn, it expands to form a red supergiant which eventually explodes in a process called supernova. The sun will also collapse in five billion years." answered the voice.

"Did you know that the sun is an integral part of the solar system?". These are the questions that gave Ananta's life meaning. Knowing almost everything and absolutely nothing at the same time - what a wonderful way to be alive.

"The Sun isn't just an ordinary star - it's the glue that holds everything together, with the help of gravity. It rotates on its axis as it revolves around the galaxy, with a tilt of 7.25 degrees. It drives ocean currents, seasons, and plant life by providing light for photosynthesis and whatnot. Without the sun, human life wouldn't even have existed.", added the Voice.

Ananta couldn't have ever imagined the importance of an ordinary star in her life. "I want to know more!" exclaimed Ananta with glistening eyes, thirsty for more knowledge.

"Is that so? Let us learn more about the solar system. In front, you will see a white door. Open it and you'll soon be transported to wherever you wish to go," answered the voice.

"Anywhere?" asked Ananta.

"Yes, anywhere," answered the voice.

"I have always wanted to know more about the solar system," said Ananta.

"Then, walk through the white door and you'll soon be transported there," replied the voice. As Ananta walked through the door, she could see the entire solar system before her - the planets revolving in their orbits with the sun in the center.

"Beautiful, isn't it? Did you know that our solar system was formed from interstellar gas and dust? The dust cloud collapsed due to shock waves emitted from a nearby collapsing star and formed a solar nebula, a spinning disc of dust material. The gravity at the center pulled the material inwards. Due to the increased pressure in the core, the hydrogen atoms combined to form helium, releasing a great amount of energy, and thus, our sun was born," the voice said.

"I could have never in a thousand years imagined this. How grand is the solar system? And oh how beautiful it is," replied Ananta with a smile on her face. She was fascinated with the information she received. "Tell me more! I want to learn more!"

"Let me tell you a little about the planets in our solar system. Jupiter is the biggest and the oldest planet in our solar system. It is the fifth planet from our sun," answered the voice.

"I also heard that it is a gas giant because they don't have hard surfaces and instead have swirling gases above a solid core. Also because they're, well, 'giants'," replied Ananta enthusiastically.

"Did you know that gas giants are also called failed stars? They contain the same basic elements as a star i.e. hydrogen and helium. However, their mass is low and isn't enough for hydrogen to fuse at the core to form a star. Saturn is another 'failed star' or gas giant," added the voice.

"Saturn is the sixth planet from the sun and the second largest planet in the solar system. It is known for its rings which are thought to be pieces of comets, asteroids, or shattered moons before they reached the planet. They are made of billions of small chunks of ice and rock coated with other materials such as dust. I also read that Saturn is the only planet in the solar system whose average density is less than that of water", exclaimed Ananta as she was happy to share what she had already learned about planets.

"I'm surprised that you know so much already! You must know about Pluto then. Tell me something about the planet", asked the voice.

"Pluto was the ninth planet in the solar system but was reclassified as a dwarf planet in 2006. Pluto has blue skies, mountains, and snow - but the snow is red!" Ananta exclaimed.

"Amazing! But are you aware of the reason why Pluto was reclassified as a dwarf planet?" asked the voice.

"Well, not really," replied Ananta.

"Let me tell you why... While Pluto was large enough to become spherical, it couldn't 'clear its neighborhood'. By this, I mean that a lot of celestial bodies of similar size orbit Pluto. Since it wasn't able to exert its orbital dominance it was reclassified as a dwarf planet", replied the voice.

"That is so interesting! But now I wish to know more about moons. In my book, I read about icy moons. Is it possible for these moons to be habitable?" Ananta was filled with a lot of doubts and she knew she could find her answers with the voice.

"Come my child, let me take you to the lunar world. Pass through the red door in front of you and you will be transported", said the voice.

"What door?" asked Ananta. Suddenly she saw a magical red door appear in front of her.

She walked through to enter another world ... the lunar world.

Chapter 3
The Lunar Serenade

Ananta landed on the barren and dusty surface of the moon. Suddenly, a robotic vehicle bumped into her.

"What is it?", asked Ananta.

"It is the Pragyan rover deployed by Chandrayan 3's Vikram lander on the south side of the moon which was sent for scientific exploration to collect invaluable scientific data," answered the voice.

Ananta remembered reading about the presence of water on the moon.

"Did you know", said the voice, "The moon has a very thin atmosphere consisting of gasses such as sodium and potassium which aren't usually found in Earth's atmosphere.

The density of the moon's atmosphere is comparable to the density of the earth's atmosphere. High energy photons and solar wind particles, chemical reactions between solar wind and lunar surface material, evaporation of surface material, and impacts of comets and meteorites are a few sources of atmosphere formation. The movement of atmospheric molecules is one of the key distinctions between the atmospheres of Earth and the moon. The velocity of the molecules is dominated by collisions between the molecules in the dense atmosphere at the surface of Earth. Atoms and molecules practically never clash on the moon due to its sparse atmosphere. Instead, they are free to travel on arcing routes that are shaped by the energy they get through the aforementioned processes as well as by the moon's gravitational pull. This kind of thin, collision-free atmosphere that reaches the ground is referred to technically as a "surface boundary exosphere." Moreover, due to its small size, the moon has a low gravity and slow escape velocity, which prevents it from retaining much of its atmosphere. The thin atmosphere of the moon is a result of the supersonic solar wind's heating of the atoms and molecules, which causes them to accelerate rapidly."

Ananta was still confused: how could she breathe on the moon if there was relatively no atmosphere?

"A few questions must go unanswered. Try to figure it out on your own," declared the voice.

Ananta looked at the moon and wondered if other moons had liquid water on their surface. Does this water exist in other forms?

"Have you ever heard of icy moons?" asked the voice.

"I've heard about them but don't know much," replied Ananta.

"Our solar system has moons that are considerably smaller than Earth but contain significantly more water! These icy moons in our solar system are nearly totally composed of water and ice. In actuality, the vast majority of the moons revolving around the outer planets—Jupiter, Saturn, Uranus, and Neptune—are icy moons.

Let's look at a few of these icy moons. Ganymede, a moon of Jupiter, is the largest moon in the solar system. Due to the size of the moon, the inner pressures are so great that high-pressure phases of ice can form, and there may even be several ocean layers sandwiched between these ice layers. The Hubble Space Telescope of NASA has discovered additional proof of an underground saltwater ocean. Jupiter's other moon, Europa, has colorful cracks that show the ocean and surface have only recently been connected. Europa has salty water, and the orange features get their color from being high in magnesium sulfate and other salts. Lenticulae, which are black spots, and chaotic terrain, which are areas of extremely broken-up ice, could also be signs of linkages between the water and the surface.

Titan, Saturn's largest moon, is a unique and amazing place. Titan has liquid hydrocarbons like methane and ethane in its rivers, lakes, seas, clouds, rain, and atmosphere. The greatest seas are hundreds of miles across and several hundred feet deep. More liquid—an ocean made primarily of water as opposed to methane—lies beneath Titan's thick water ice layer.

The largest of Neptune's satellites, Triton, is one of the few known objects in the solar system to have an atmosphere primarily composed of nitrogen. Triton is the only satellite in the solar system known to have a surface mostly composed of nitrogen ice because it is so cold that most of its nitrogen is condensed as frost. The pinkish deposits make up a sizable south polar cap that is thought to include methane ice, which when exposed to sunlight would have reacted to generate pink or red compounds. It is thought that the dark streaks covering these pink ices are large geyser-like plumes of icy and maybe carbonaceous dust," the voice went on and on about icy moons.

However, Ananta interrupted it by asking, "If these icy moons have several layers of ice and beneath these layers of salt water, is it possible that life may exist on these moons or other planets?"

The Voice paused for a moment and then answered, "Some of these moons are promising destinations for finding life. Planetary habitability is the measure of a planet's or a natural satellite's potential to develop and sustain life. Let me take you to a planet in our solar system - Mars to understand more about habitability."

As Ananta walked into the blue door appearing on the horizon, she was transported into another world.

Chapter 4
The Martian Chronicles

In the dark of the night, Mars, a rusted jewel, whispered in its sandy embrace tales of ancient winds and time-carved canyons. A reddish planet in the night sky, like a rusty desert it has rocky hills and canyons all over its surface. Ananta could not believe her eyes. She finally had the opportunity to see the planet she had heard about all her life.

"Did you know that although Mars lies in the habitable zone, it still isn't habitable in the current stages?" asked the voice.

Ananta, bewildered by this statement, asked, "How is that even possible?".

The Voice began, "The habitable zone is also known as the Goldilocks zone. Essentially, it is a region around a star where an orbiting planet can host liquid water. Because planets orbiting at that "just right" distance from a star are neither too hot nor too cold to support liquid water, the habitable zone is also referred to as the "Goldilocks zone." The water on planets either turns to steam or freezes depending on how close or how far they are from their star. Mars doesn't lie in this zone and it is unlikely that life exists here in the present."

"Why is that?", interrupted Ananta.

"The low atmosphere on Mars makes it difficult for liquid water to remain stable on the surface, which is one of the main obstacles to Mars being a habitable planet. The absence of a robust magnetosphere, which would have shielded the atmosphere from the solar wind, is considered to be a major factor in why Mars' atmosphere is so thin. More than 95% of the atmosphere of the Red Planet is made up of carbon dioxide, and fewer than 1% of it is oxygen. The lack of an atmosphere on Mars makes it vulnerable to collisions from meteorites, asteroids, and comets. Moreover, Mars experiences temperatures ranging from a frigid -195°F (-125°C) in winter to a relatively warmer 70°F (20°C) in some equatorial regions during summer. These are a few factors that make Mars inhabitable in the current stages. However, there is a possibility that life may have existed on this red planet in the past. Mars might have had a denser atmosphere which would allow water to flow and microbial life to thrive."

Ananta, overwhelmed by the flood of information, struggled to grasp its entirety.

"Let me take you to another extreme planet, Venus," said the voice.

Venus, often called Earth's "sister planet," shined brilliantly, its thick atmosphere trapping scorching heat and hiding a hostile surface beneath swirling clouds of sulfuric acid.

"Venus, by many standards, is the most extreme world in our neighborhood. At the surface, the planet's hazardous environment is compressed to 90 times the pressure at sea level, or about equivalent to an ocean depth of 900 meters, and is seasoned with sulfuric acid. The highest recorded temperature of Venus is 900 degrees Fahrenheit (482 degrees Celsius). The atmosphere is comprised mostly of carbon dioxide with clouds composed of sulfuric acid. The heated, high-pressure carbon dioxide acts corrosively at the surface. The lack of a liquid iron core and the sluggish rotation of Venus prevents the creation of a powerful magnetic dynamo, which is the main reason for the planet's lack of a magnetic field. Venus' core is assumed to be mostly solid which is in sharp contrast to Earth's. This makes it more difficult to build a magnetic barrier to defend the planet. However, Venus has an induced magnetic field generated by the interaction of the sun's magnetic field and the planet's outer atmosphere. Due to the absence of a global magnetic field, Venus is more susceptible to cosmic radiation, potentially posing a higher level of radiation exposure for any future manned missions. Several rovers have been sent to Venus but the majority of them burnt down shortly after landing on the surface of the planet. These inhospitable conditions make it highly challenging for any form of life as we know it to exist on Venus."

"What about the other planets of the solar system? Are there any possibilities that life may exist in our neighborhood?", Ananta's curiosity was insatiable and her mind ever inquisitive.

"Well, perhaps that's an adventure for another day".

Ananta was confused by what that meant. Suddenly, there was a bright white light and Ananta got sucked into it..

Chapter 5
Jupiter's Celestial Ballet

Awestruck by Jupiter's swirling storms, colossal bands, and vibrant hues, Ananta floats around the gas giant, for there is no true solid surface on Jupiter. She was confused yet mesmerized at the same time.

"The planet's primary constituents are hydrogen and helium gas. As you journey further inside the planet, pressure and temperatures rise, eventually reaching so intense that electrons are thought to be separated from their hydrogen atoms.", said the voice. "That immense pressure also compresses hydrogen gases into liquid form, resulting in a vast ocean completely composed of liquid hydrogen."

"That's quite interesting. However, does Jupiter support life?" interrupted Ananta.

The planet's atmosphere is characterized by extreme temperatures, high levels of radiation, and powerful storms. The top layer of clouds is composed of ammonia and methane. These conditions are extremely inhospitable to life as we understand it. It also has a powerful magnetic field and far more intense radiation belts than Earth. Jupiter is not a suitable setting for life as we know it due to its severe circumstances." "Well, what about its icy moons? Are there any possibilities of the existence of life there?" questioned Ananta. "Jupiter's icy moons, such as Europa, Ganymede, and Callisto, have long piqued scientists' interest in the possibility of life beyond Earth. Europa is especially significant because it has a subterranean ocean under its frozen exterior. This ocean is thought to hold more than twice as much water as Earth, boosting the prospect of a viable habitat for life. Scientists believe that hydrothermal vents on the ocean floor may contain the chemical elements and energy sources required to support microscopic life. Recent studies from satellite missions have revealed persuasive evidence of water plumes erupting from Europa, implying that material from the moon's deep ocean may reach the moon's surface. Exploration of these frozen moons has considerable promise for shedding insight on the possible habitability of these distant worlds and the presence of alien life in our own solar system.", answered the voice. Fascinated, Ananta pondered about the existence of life on planets outside the solar system. Could it be possible? "My child", the voice started speaking, "we have already explored a few planets which are not capable of harboring life currently. Nevertheless, it is quite possible that these planets might host life in the future. Anything is possible in the realm of space. Now, let me take you to an exoplanet - Kepler 452B, to learn more about habitability." A doorway opened and Ananta was transported to the constellation of Cygnus, where this exoplanet lay. Would her questions be answered this time?

Chapter 6

Kepler 452B: A Super Earth's Tale

Ananta found herself in the constellation of Cygnus, surrounded by the ethereal glow of distant stars. The cosmic symphony of twinkling lights created a mesmerizing backdrop as Ananta's gaze fixed upon a massive blue door that stood before her, seemingly out of place amidst the celestial beauty. It beckoned her, its azure hue radiating an otherworldly allure that stirred her sense of adventure.

With a mixture of trepidation and excitement, Ananta approached the colossal door. It bore no markings or symbols, yet an unspoken invitation lingered in the air. As she extended her hand to touch the cold surface, the door creaked open, revealing a passage to the unknown. A rush of anticipation filled her as she crossed the threshold into an alien world.

The transition was seamless, and Ananta found herself standing on the surface of Kepler-452b. The landscape unfolded like a cosmic canvas, bathed in the warm glow of its parent star. The scenery mirrored Earth, from rolling hills to vast oceans, creating an uncanny sense of déjà vu. Ananta's senses absorbed the familiarity, igniting a profound connection between her and this distant exoplanet.

Kepler-452b, nestled perfectly within its star's habitable zone, boasted a size comparable to Earth. Its potential for liquid water intrigued Ananta, prompting her to explore the planet's secrets. As she traversed the terrain, she marveled at the delicate balance of cosmic elements that allowed for such Earth-like conditions.

Guided by an unspoken force, Ananta found herself pondering the similarities between Kepler-452b's sun and Earth's sun. The voice of her curiosity questioned the universe, seeking to understand the intricacies that could sustain life in this far-off realm. It was a journey into the heart of astrophysics, a quest to unravel the cosmic threads that wove the tapestry of habitability.

Inquisitive by nature, Ananta sought answers from an unseen presence, a voice resonating in the vastness of space. She questioned the concept of habitability, eager to grasp its meaning in the context of celestial bodies. The voice, a cosmic guide, explained that habitability was the measure of a celestial body's potential to develop and sustain life.

Ananta absorbed the wisdom imparted by the voice, delving into the essential factors that defined habitability. Distance from the star, a stable rotational axis, the presence of tectonic plates, the right amount of water, a breathable atmosphere, and a protective magnetic field – each element played a crucial role in a planet's ability to support life.

Kepler-452b, it seemed, performed a delicate dance orchestrated by cosmic forces. Ananta marveled at the intricate interplay of these elements, realizing the rarity of such conditions in the vastness of the universe. The realization deepened her appreciation for Earth's unique status as a cradle of life.

As the cosmic tour continued, the voice revealed a mysterious blue door, standing in stark contrast to the vibrant landscape. It was a portal to an inhospitable place, a celestial anomaly that both fascinated and frightened Ananta – the black hole. Despite a momentary hesitation, her insatiable curiosity propelled her forward, urging her to uncover the secrets hidden within the extremes of the cosmos.

Ananta approached the mysterious blue door, her heartbeat echoing in the cosmic silence. With a determined breath, she opened the door, revealing a vortex of darkness that seemed to defy the laws of physics. The voice accompanied her, offering guidance as they stepped into the gravitational embrace of the black hole.

The transition was surreal, with space-time bending and distorting around them. Ananta observed the gradual shift from the familiar cosmic scenery to an abstract mosaic of colors and shapes. The voice explained the intricacies of the black hole, detailing its singularity and event horizon.

As they delved deeper, Ananta's senses were overwhelmed by the intense gravitational forces and the surreal phenomena occurring around the event horizon. The voice elucidated the impossibility of life as we know it thriving in such an environment, where the very fabric of reality seemed to unravel.

Yet, the exploration didn't stop at the exterior. The voice hinted at the mysterious interior of the black hole, a realm where the laws of physics ceased to hold sway. Ananta, fueled by a blend of curiosity and trepidation, questioned the nature of this enigmatic space.

The voice's responses were shrouded in cosmic ambiguity. The black hole's interior remained an uncharted territory, a cosmic frontier where speculation ranged from the existence of alternate universes to the possibility of a gateway to the unknown. Ananta, standing at the precipice of the cosmic abyss, contemplated the uncertainties that lay ahead.

The discussion veered towards the existential nature of the universe, prompting Ananta to question the voice about the meaning of life in the grand cosmic scheme. The voice, with a wisdom derived from eons of existence, spoke of the cyclical nature of creation and destruction, emphasizing that every celestial body, including life itself, had a beginning and an end.

As Ananta gazed into the unfathomable depths of the black hole, the voice's words resonated in her mind. Life, it seemed, was a fleeting yet profound journey. The voice encouraged her to embrace the uncertainty, to find purpose in the continual pursuit of knowledge and growth.

A moment of profound introspection enveloped Ananta as she hovered on the threshold of the cosmic abyss. The beauty of life, she realized, lay not only in its certainties but in the vast realm of unknown possibilities. With newfound determination, she allowed herself to be drawn into the heart of the black hole, the cosmic forces swirling around her.

Chapter 7
Voyage to the Cosmic Abyss

Ananta stepped out of the colossal blue door and
found herself on the outskirts of a colossal black hole. Its
gravitational pull was so intense that it distorted the very fabric
of space and time around it. The voice, a steady companion,
guided her through an exploration of the black hole's
structure, shedding light on the singularity – a point of infinite
density – and the event horizon – the boundary beyond
which nothing, not even light, could escape.

Black holes owed their existence to the remnants of a larger
star which might have died in a Supernova explosion.
The extreme conditions surrounding the black hole fascinated
Ananta. However, curiosity sparked questions about the
possibility of life in such an environment. The voice explained
that while planets might form around a black hole, the intense
gravitational forces and radiation made it inhospitable for life

as we know it. Ananta, absorbing this cosmic knowledge, felt a sense of awe and insignificance in the vastness of the universe.

The discussion then delved into the mysterious interior of the black hole. The voice, usually a well of information, admitted that the structure remained an enigma and stated that one does not know of what happens inside- one might die or live forever and enter into another UNIVERSE. Ananta's mind raced with possibilities – from life-ending scenarios to the potential for eternal existence. The voice reminded her that uncertainty was an inherent part of exploration and should not deter the pursuit of knowledge.

As Ananta pondered the uncertainties of life and the universe, she was intrigued by the phenomenon of life culminating into death. The voice shared a profound truth: everything, including life, had a beginning and an end. The essence of the journey lay in the growth and exploration along the way. Ananta, amidst the cosmic wonders, contemplated the transient nature of existence.

In a moment of revelation, Ananta gazed into the heart of the black hole. The swirling cosmic dance seemed to reflect the ebb and flow of life. The voice, sensing her contemplation, encouraged her to embrace the beauty of the process – the journey of learning and growing.

With newfound determination, Ananta decided to delve deeper. The infinite possibilities within the uncertainties of existence beckoned her. The voice, with a final piece of wisdom, urged Ananta to continue learning and growing, echoing in her mind as she allowed herself to be drawn into the heart of the black hole.

Abruptly, Ananta awakened in her room. The familiar

surroundings and the soft play of Neil deGrasse Tyson's podcast in the background grounded her. A profound sense of purpose filled her being. She joined her family for dinner, the open book of astrophysics on the table serving as a reminder of her unyielding passion for the cosmos.

Ananta reflected on the journey through the black hole – a journey that transcended the boundaries of space and time. The experiences, whether challenging or awe-inspiring, contributed to the beauty of life's narrative. The cosmos, with its mysteries and wonders, became the canvas upon which her insatiable curiosity painted a vivid and ever-expanding story.

In the quiet moments of the night, Ananta revisited the lessons from the black hole. Life's uncertainties, like the cosmic unknowns, were part of the grand tapestry. Every question, every challenge, and every moment of growth added color to the intricate design of her journey.

With a heart filled with gratitude and a mind buzzing with cosmic revelations, Ananta embraced the beauty of the unknown. The next morning, she woke up with the same passion, ready to embark on new cosmic explorations. The blue door might have closed, but the echoes of the black hole lingered, a constant reminder of the infinite possibilities that awaited her in the universe.

Chapter 8
The Cosmic Awakening

Twenty years had passed since her travel through the solar system with Neil Tyson. Now, standing before a sea of eager faces at a prestigious convocation ceremony, she had become a luminary in the field of astrophysics. The auditorium buzzed with anticipation as she began her speech, carefully alluding to the cosmic secret she had guarded for so long.

Her narrative unfolded like a celestial tapestry, weaving the threads of her journey through the vast expanse of the universe. As she delved into the intricacies of her research, a hushed excitement filled the air. The story of her encounter with the black hole, a story she had kept veiled in the shroud of scientific restraint, hung in the atmosphere like a tantalizing mystery.

"I stand before you today as a humble explorer of the

cosmos," she began, her voice carrying the weight of both scientific rigor and a deeply personal odyssey.

She continued, "Two decades ago, I found myself on the precipice of the unknown, gazing into the unfathomable depths of a black hole. What I saw, the secrets I unearthed, have fueled my passion for unraveling the mysteries of the universe."

Her words wove a spell, transporting the audience through the corridors of space and time. The young girls seated in the front rows listened with wide-eyed wonder, their dreams taking flight on the wings of her narrative. They were the torchbearers of a new generation inspired by her indomitable spirit and insatiable curiosity.

"I won't divulge the specifics of what lay within that cosmic abyss," she continued, casting a knowing smile to the audience.

"Some mysteries are meant to endure, to spark the imagination and propel us forward into the uncharted territories of knowledge. The beauty of science lies in its ability to transform the enigmatic into the understandable, the unknowable into the known."

The crowd hung on her every word, and the atmosphere in the auditorium vibrated with intellectual fervor. As she recounted the challenges, the breakthroughs, and the moments of sheer awe that punctuated her career, she cast a spotlight on the collective journey of humanity's exploration of the cosmos.

Turning her attention to the young girls in the front rows, she acknowledged their presence with a genuine warmth that resonated through the hall. "To the aspiring astrophysicists in our midst, especially the young women who sit before me, know this: the universe is vast, and within its cosmic dance, countless mysteries are awaiting your discovery. Embrace the unknown with courage, and let your curiosity be the compass guiding you through the realms of the stars."

The applause that erupted from the audience was thunderous, echoing the sentiment that had taken root in the hearts of those present.

One young girl, her eyes alight with inspiration, stood and proclaimed, "You've not only expanded our understanding of the cosmos but have ignited a passion in us to follow in your footsteps." The cheers that followed were a symphony of gratitude and determination, a testament to the transformative power of one woman's journey through the cosmos.

As she concluded her speech, she left the stage with a sense of fulfillment, knowing that her story had become a beacon, lighting the way for those who dared to gaze into the unknown and dream of reaching for the stars.

Acknowledgements

This incredible journey would have been inconceivable without the steadfast support of **my parents**, who have consistently urged me to explore the realms of knowledge through reading and questioning. My sincere appreciation extends to **my teachers** for their unwavering inspiration and support. I am profoundly grateful to all those who played a pivotal role in shaping this book—be it through the meticulous process of editing, the creative touch of illustrations, or the intricate steps of publishing.

My heartfelt thanks go out to the scientific community and mentors whose invaluable contributions have unveiled the profound mysteries of the universe, whether through captivating podcasts, enlightening research papers, or other impactful published works.

A special acknowledgment is reserved for **Sir Neil deGrasse Tyson**, whose inspiration has fueled my deep dive into the enigmatic cosmos.

I carry an eternal debt of gratitude to each individual who has been part of this transformative journey, contributing to the realization of my thoughts and the creation of this book.

www.ingramcontent.com/pod-product-compliance
Lightning Source LLC
Chambersburg PA
CBHW021815150726
47989CB00004B/1937